Unless a person is explicitly identified by name, the statements that are used should not be directly attributed to any specific person.

Unless otherwise marked, all scripture quotations are referenced from the King James Version of the Bible.

ISBN-10: 0982700164
ISBN-13: 978-0-9827001-6-7

Printed in the United States of America.
Published by Kingdom Journey Press
A Division of Kingdom Journey Enterprises, Woodbridge, VA
www.kjpressinc.com

Cover Design by Brand U, Inc.

METRO TALK

A Series of Public Service Announcements and Words of Encouragement to Help Jumpstart Your Day

From the Mind of

Eugene Hagood

Kingdom Journey Press
A Division of Kingdom Journey Enterprises
Woodbridge, VA

“Metro Talk” is a series of Public Service Announcements, filled with lots of humor, and Words of Encouragement to help jumpstart your day – hee hee hee!!!

A merry heart doeth good like a medicine: but a broken spirit drieth the bones.

Proverbs 17:22

Dedication

To the loving memory of my mother,
***ARDELIA GLADYS-JUNE HAGOOD**……*
Rest In Peace my angel and thank you for instilling in me
the virtues that are now being manifested in my life!!!
I will always love you!☺

Acknowledgements

First giving honor to God for ALL HE has done for me thus far. I cannot express enough how thankful, blessed, loved and humbled I am for what the Master has done with an old wretch like me.

Some days I just marvel at how I got to this point or that point in my life and at the head of everything I do, God is first and foremost!! So many of you mean so much to me and have been here with me through the unemployment, the breakdowns, and the ups/downs of life, and you have never let me stop believing in God or His grace and mercy, nor stop believing in me. So whether you are reading this or your name is mentioned in my book, I need you all to know that I love you and don't ever doubt that.....God bless you all!

To my Family (Vessels and Powells): I have been so blessed to be a member of such a loving, caring and God-fearing family. I want to take this opportunity to thank each of you for your love, understanding and guidance over the years, which has assisted me in growing up and becoming the man that I am today, so know that I love you and pray God's continued blessings upon you!!! ☺

I would like to acknowledge some of the SPECIAL PEOPLE in my life and thank them for the encouragement, love, guidance and laughter over the years. Facebook has been an amazing outlet for me and was the catalyst for "Metro Talk", so I want to thank my FACEBOOK FAMILY and some people in particular who have uplifted me and have truly been blessings to me and my life: Keisha Tyson-Cook, Tonia Moore, Anthony Jones, Princess Gunter, Daryl Daniels, Nina Baker, Joya Joyner-Countiss, Chester Waters, LaShan Haynes, Karen Hall-Ross, Alisa Burgess, Kim Breedlove-Parker, Ivorie Fisher (love you cuzin), Denise M.

Walker, Sonya Kitchens, Delmarie Hines, Levette Crawford-Thomas, Tiffany Burns, Matrice Hopson, Crystal Taylor-Dixon, Madeline Harris-Farrell, Ernest M. Phillips, Brandye' Scott, Tammy Coleman, Sheldon Morris (my future "Wipeout" partner), Kathy Smith, Sonja Vessels, Christie Seymour, Kathy Unzicker-Byrd, Leah Unzicker-Dargan, Debora Royal, Cynthia Wellington-Washington, Regina Williams-Watts, Gwen Bently-Collins, Lori White-Lyons, Yolanda Jones, Mildred Allen, DeMargo Hopson (my Big Bruddah), Sheldon "Corey" Vessels, Cynthia Boxberger and Family, Cynthia Gause-Howell, Keith Overton, and Tia Nichols.

To my ANGELS AND BOSLEY: SHARON VESSELS, KHALIAH WHITTINGTON, TRENA BLAKE-CLARKE AND LEONARD RANDOLPH, JR. AND I AM "CHARLIE".....hee-hee-hee!!!! Each morning, this group of FAMILY gathers via e-mail, text messages or phone calls and we talk all day, everyday....hee-hee-hee!! We have loved, encouraged, guided, consoled and some days chastised each other over the years and I know that I would not be in this position without God and the presence of each of you in my life, so here is my sincere, heart-felt thanks to each of you for loving me through it all ....let us continue supporting one another because there is much more greatness for each of us! I love each of you with all of my heart.....God bless you!!

To my BFF Renee Allen......WE have been BEST FRIENDS for almost 30 years and I have enjoyed every minute of it. You are and have always been an inspiration to me, my muse on many occasions and my guardian when I tended to get out of line....hee-hee-hee!!! Through the years, we have grown so much as individuals, but one thing remains common.....Our love for God and one another!!! I love you BFF (now can I have my VISA debit card back since I gave you a shout out?)…haaaaaaaaaaaaaaaa!!! Just kidding, I truly love you Sweetie!☺

To my Lil Brother Daryl Daniels, my Lil Sister LaShan Haynes and my Big Sister Denise Walker…….Thank each of you for being in my life and loving me unconditionally (I know some days were hard….hee-hee-hee), but I cherish and adore each of you and thank God for your presence in my life!☺

SPECIAL THANKS TO THE POINTER/GILLUM FAMILIES – Your love has touched my life and saved me on many days and I can never say "Thank You" enough……I LOVE YOU!!

SPECIAL-SPECIAL THANKS TO THE MARSHALL FAMILY –I have never been more honored to be a part of such a loving and caring family!!! R.I.P. Momma Mary Marshall…..love you Angel ☺

Honorable Mention to Casandra Johnson of Kingdom Journey Press Publishing Company for having the vision to see this project through and believing in ME to make a difference….thank you sister and God bless you. ☺

Introduction

"Metro Talk" was borne almost three years ago from my experiences while traveling on the public transportation system in the Washington-Metropolitan area. Each day I would enter the Metro system and some of the sights, sounds and yes, smells would make me laugh, shake my head and even cringe, so I began sharing such encounters on Facebook, hence the name "Metro Talk".

As the years have gone by, I have gained quite a following of people who wait each morning for me to post "Metro Talk" and make them laugh or jump start their days, so I hope that this book will do just that….JUMP START YOUR DAY AND POSSIBLY INSPIRE YOU IN SOME WAY!!

May God bless you and continue to use me as a blessing to make others smile, laugh and be an inspiration. I am not a perfect person, but I strive to be the BEST person that I can be. You can have FAITH and still have FUN.

Table of Contents

Father God, today I choose to focus on You. I bless and praise You no matter what my circumstances look like!!! This should be MY prayer EVERY DAY!!!!

Good Morning Family.....have a blessed day!!!

METRO TALK

by

Eugene Hagood

Morning Family

Good Morning…GOD never said the journey would be EASY, but He did say that the arrival would be WORTHWHILE.

TGIF = Thank God I'm Favored, so give thanks!

Morning Family.....I am on the Metro and this feeling of complete PEACE has overcome me and tears are flowing.....when I think of the goodness of the Lord and ALL HE HAS DONE FOR ME, MY SOUL SCREAMS "YES, YES, YES"!

Luv you my Family!

Morning Family….Have you ever heard a song that takes you back to lost love, that person you just knew was THE ONE, but it didn't work out? That's where I am right now.....I know things happen for a REASON and I refuse to stop believing in TRUE LOVE....I JUST CANNOT!!

Metro Talk

"Metro Talk"....standing on platform and lady just cuts in front of me, so I am looking around like "no she didn't" and guy next to me is laughing, so I begin praying out loud "Lord, order my steps, give me patience to deal with RUDE people, and let me not smack this lady in the head with this Kindle....IN JESUS NAME I PRAY, AMEN."

When I open my eyes, the guy and I are alone.....PRAYER WORKS...hee hee hee!!

Morning Family!

"Metro Talk"....WARNING: Bullying will not be tolerated on the Metro!! A lady was in such a hurry to board the train today that she pushed past me and several others, SO I said "Dang, are you driving the train or something?" She says, "Thought you'll weren't moving." Another patron scoffs at her comment and I say “I don’t need you to think for me”…..GOOD DAY MISS, I SAID GOOD DAY!!!

Morning Family!

"Metro Talk".....dude enters train and STOPS right inside door WITH rolling briefcase and reading an e-reader....SMH!! Come on dude, this isn't an Internet cafe; we're trying to board the train. He replies "It's a Kindle" and I say "Well KINDLY move so we can get on the train....read when the doors close"....hee hee hee!! (Humming "Jesus Be a Fence")

Morning Family!

"Metro Talk".....on the back of the bus in Crystal City minding my business and lady saunters to the back and just stands, so I pay her nooch....she proceeds to SQUEEZE between me and the pole. I look at her and say, "I know it is "HUMP" day, but if you are going to nearly sit on my lap, MY NAME IS GENE AND I AM AN AQUARIUS"….hee-hee-hee!!! She gasps then laughs!!!

Morning Family!!

"Metro Talk"….PSA: Ladies, if you insist on carrying those HUGE purses that are like lawn/leaf bags with straps, PLEASE be mindful of the patrons around you who are being BEAT UP by your big purse!! YOU HAVE BEEN WARNED.....this war will NOT be televised, so beware "Metro Talk" is coming for you.....hee hee hee!!

Morning Family!

"Metro Talk".....have you ever walked behind someone who swings their arms so wide that you can't get past? This is my fate at L'Enfant Plaza and the train is approaching. Unable to maneuver around her, I say "Excuse me "Robocop", but can I get by?".....hee hee hee!! She swirls around and just as she begins to speak, I hit her with the signature.....GOOD DAY MISS, I SAID GOOD DAY!!

Morning Family

"Metro Talk"......this must be "Obstacle Tuesday" as I keep winding up walking behind this lady "wobbling" in high heels...SMH!! Ghurl, if you have not mastered walking in heels, then play "Dress Up Barbie" on your own time....NOW MOOOOVE before I drop a banana peel....hee hee hee!!

Morning Family

"Metro Talk"......train doors open and folks scrambling for seats, so this lady tries to race me to a seat and in my mind I am saying "Not today Punkin", so I weave and scoot into the seat and she is HEATED...hee hee hee!! She is glaring at me from across the aisle right now......!! Maybe I should offer her a piece of gum......GOOD DAY MISS, I SAID GOOD DAY…hee-hee-hee!!!

“Metro Talk"....PSA: LADIES, THE METRO IS NOT THE VENUE TO TAKE OUT YOUR BRAIDS/TRACKS!! Excuse me, but I don't want them scraps and flakes on MY clothes....I CAN'T BEWEAVE THE NERVE OF YOU.....hee hee hee!!

Morning Family!

"Metro Talk".....lady holding up line at turn stall rubbing card back/forth on sensor and gate won't open. Finally the Station Manager comes out and tells her there is no money on the card. HELLO, the machine told you that and now it's laughing at you like I am.....!!

Morning Family!

"Metro Talk".....lady comments about men getting pedicures/manicures (I have on sandals today) and asks if I get pedicures (Sometimes), but lotion is the key....I look down at her feet and her nail polish is chipped, so I comment "I take it that YOU don't though?" She stammers "I have an appt. today." HAVE A GOOD DAY MISS!!

"Metro Talk".....Dude on train is wearing a winter skully hat and sweating profusely!! I want to snatch it off his head and say "Look at a calendar, IT'S SUMMER.....hee hee hee!! Older lady offered him a Kleenex..... Lawd these kids!!

"Metro Talk"….Dang it's HOT at Southern Avenue Metro....where are the ushers with the fans like in church when the air goes out?....hee hee hee!!

Morning Family! :)

"Metro Talk".....What is the deal with folks on escalators? When they come to the end, they just STOP!! MOOOOOVVVVVEEEEE, the floor ain't moving.....hee hee hee!! If I fall, I am taking 1 or 2 of you'll with me....TRUST AND BELIEVE.....!!

Morning Family! :)

“Metro Talk”….RIDDLE ME THIS: If someone almost knocks me down rushing for the subway am I still obligated to be a gentleman and allow them to board the train in front of me when the train FINALLY comes? Come on Family, you all KNOW ME....what do you think I did/said to this person? This should be hilarious.....HAPPY "FUNNY" WEDNESDAY :)

In the Midst of It All....Smile

Want to say THANK YOU to all my FB Family for the love and support yesterday.....man, I was in such a dark place and even though I love Batman movies, I AM NOT TRYING TO BE THE DARK KNIGHT....!!! I think of myself more as the Riddler or the Joker...hee-hee-hee!!! Good Morning Family....have a blessed day and know that God loves you and so do I.....Smile!!!

Just finished my new workout as prescribed by my co-worker/personal trainer.....LORD, IF BEAUTY IS PAIN, I SHOULD LOOK LIKE A PRO WRESTLER, OR AT THIS STAGE IN THE GAME, I WOULD SETTLE FOR A PRO BOWLER (if he was slim)....hee-hee-hee!!! Morning Family....maybe raining outside, but GOD'S LOVE is shining on the inside...have a blessed day...Smile!!!

Sitting at my desk and listening to "The Best of the Winans".......man, the song "TOMORROW" brings tears to MY eyes!!! When I hear that song and "CAN YOU REACH MY FRIEND" by Helen Baylor.....the floodgates are open because I can relate to the meaning of both songs.....THANK YOU LORD FOR YOUR GRACE AND MERCY AND FOR SAVING A WRETCH LIKE ME.......Smile!

Thinking that I really need to get serious about living healthier......as I sit here at my desk brushing glazed doughnut crumbs off my sweater.....hee-hee-hee!!!!! Maybe I should have gotten some 2% milk instead of that Arizona Mango juice....LMBO!!! Good Morning Family....have a "Warm Wednesday" (the weekend is almost here....thank ya!!!)…Smile!

Some of my experiences on the Metro have not been so funny, like the time when I was suffering with severe abdominal pain on my way to a doctor's appointment and I collapsed right on the concourse. As I laid there writhing in pain, all I could see were people's feet moving around me and NO ONE would help me. Finally a young man stopped and asked could he help me and called for an ambulance. When I made it to the ER, I was diagnosed with a bleeding hernia. These next few quotes were during that time before and after my hernia surgery.........

Finally home from spending most of the day in the ER at Georgetown Hospital....the devil is trying to attack me in several areas of MY life as well, but my family and I REFUSE TO GIVE HIM THE VICTORY!!! I just think what MY life would be without FAITH and I know I would not be where I am today....pray for ME as I pray for YOU Family...Good night!! I sing "I Got the Victory" as I drift off to sleep...smile!!!

So thankful for the Prayer Warriors out there and my FB Family....LOVE YOU ALL!!! I go for consultation for my surgery today at 2:00 pm, so I will keep you all updated....again thanks for loving, caring, supporting and encouraging ME.....God has blessed me with such an amazing family and I thank you all....Smile!!!!

On my way to George Washington University Hospital for my CAT Scan.....I wonder if they will find Nemo?.....hee hee hee!! Morning my Fam....Smile!!

Inspiration during my recovery…….

Morning Family....feeling GREAT today!!! Although I awoke this morning to the news of gun violence in DC and families suffering with loss of loved ones, I am so thankful for God's GRACE AND MERCY. I will pray for YOU as you pray for ME because the FAMILY THAT PRAYS TOGETHER STAYS TOGETHER....Smile!!!

During my recuperation, I still reached out to my FB Family and GOD.....

I am here to report that I am recovering nicely albeit slowly (still tenderness and soreness), but things are going well. I just wanted to let you all know how much I appreciate you and truly thank God daily for your presence in my life.

God bless and love you...Smile!!!

Recovery is over……back to work

Morning Family...today marks the end of my home recuperating…back to work tomorrow...ugh!!! I know one thing, if I don't wash these loads of clothes, they will see me in the office in swimming trunks, dress socks and "I Love Ocean City" t-shirt...hee-hee-hee!!! Have a great day my FAM! Smile!!!

Feeling like a homeless person trying to push this cart down the stairs of my apartment building because I can't lift anything over 10 pounds and my laundry bag weighs more than that, I think.....Lord don't let this cart fall over and my dirty clothes be all over the hallway....hee-hee-hee!!! Don't think my neighbors will like to find dirty clothes on their mailbox....hee-hee-hee!!!

Relapse on the Metro……

My doctor had suggested that I could return to work in a week, but he nor I took into account that although I look in my mid-30's (no comments....Percocet withdrawal), my body definitely KNOWS it's rightful age and was not ready for such an undertaking....hee-hee-hee!!!

Hello Family/Friends,

I would like to thank each of you for your thoughts, prayers, prepared meals, cards/e-cards and most importantly LOVE during my surgery and subsequent recovery. I must tell you that I truly underestimated the severity of my surgery and proceeded to go back to work this past Tuesday......BOY, WAS THAT THE WRONG DECISION!!!

Leave something for GOD, but don't leave GOD for something because in life, something will always leave YOU, but GOD will ALWAYS be there....author unknown!! Morning Family....God bless you all and HAPPY FRIDAY....Smile!!!!

I know that God is truly working with me TODAY....between the co-worker taking my food off my desk and then having to ride the "Soul Train" this morning like a sardine where this guy was so close to my face his breath was burning my nostrils....hee-hee-hee!!!! Through ALL that, I did not cuss, I did not spit nor GO OFF.....now those who TRULY KNOW ME....tell me God ain't good....Smile!!!!

Truly understand that NOTHING happens by chance....God has surrounded ME with ANGELS that I call FAMILY!! I MAY NOT HAVE MUCH, BUT ONE THING I KNOW THAT I KNOW IS THAT I HAVE LOVE IN MY LIFE....Smile!! All else is a bonus.... Good Night Family! :)

Waffling back and forth with feeling down in my spirit then uplifted...what is that about? Some days knowing that the enemy is trying to take you down, it is still hard to pull myself out of that valley....thank you Family for being here for me, allowing me to express myself and for LOVING ME unconditionally....Smile!!

Want to start off by saying.....HALLELUJAH!!!! I logged on FB this morning and four of my Family had status posts that touched me all the way to my toes, then on top of that I'm playing my Marvin Sapp CD.....TODAY IS GOING TO BE A MARVELOUS DAY....I am stomping the devil's head as I type.....almost forgot....GOOD MORNING FAMILY AND KNOW THAT GOD LOVES YOU AND SO DO I….SMILE!!!

While on My Journey

Walking to the Giant in Eastover and young mother is pulling her daughter down the street yelling "Why do you keep falling down?".....uhhh probably because she has on footie pajamas and you put sandals on her feet too.....hee hee hee!! Little girl yelling "My feet Mommy, my feet"!!! Why me Lord....!!

HAPPY 4TH WEEKEND FAMILY! :)

Cracking up laughing....folks are funny. I am at PEPCO paying a bill, this lady is racing me to get to the window first....you know she tripped and had the nerve to glare at ME....I didn't trip you, blame Payless....hee hee hee!!

COMCAST tech came out to install wireless modem and had the nerve to hint to me for a tip for his hard labor...LOL. Dude, here is a granola bar, bottle water and Pennysaver to find you a new job....GOOD DAY SIR.....hee hee hee!!!

SMH....why can't folks just let you mind your own business? Guy is talking to me and I am just staring at him. He says "Why are you looking at me like that?" I reply "Was I talking to you and didn't realize it?" He says "I don't think so" and I say "Then why are YOU talking to me about something that doesn't concern either one of us?" Good day Sir, I said GOOD DAY!!!....hee-hee-hee!!!

SMH and giggling.....Credit Union called me to tell me my credit card payment was late last month and how I should pay it before the date to avoid finance charges. I told him "Why don't you pay the bill off and I will pay YOU back with no finance charges"....hee-hee-hee!!!! He stuttered and I said "Good day Sir, I SAID GOOD DAY"....!!!

Wassup Family :)

Back at the Office

SMH.....a person walked by my desk and saw that I had some Girl Scout Cookies in my desk drawer, not eating them, just in my drawer and commented that they were bad for my health....I replied, "Being nosey is bad for your health too".....(end scene)....hee-hee-hee!!!!

My good friend Cynthia Wellington Washington said it best "halter tops, daisy dukes, flip-flops, & wife-beaters are not a good look in a professional office setting". DON'T WEAR HALTER TOPS WITH WINGS ON YOUR BACK....This is NOT an audition for the new "Batman" movie....hee-hee-hee!!!! I know my limitations....know yours....!!

More Metro Talk

"Metro Talk"…. After being nearly knocked down the stairs by this woman running for the train, I stood on the platform for the next train and she began trying to get in front of me like I was supposed to let her on (usually allow females to get on first), so I body blocked her and said "Don't even try it....GIT BACK"!!!! She mean mugged me all the way to L'Enfant Plaza and I LAUGHED ALL THE WAY!!!!

"Metro Talk"…..is SMH....Why do people stand right at the door when waiting for the elevator?.....dang woman scared the mess out of me when the door opened..... hee hee hee!!

"Metro Talk".....We are raised to respect our elders, but if MY nana leaves the house with leggings, tight shirt and all-gray cornrows.....I am taking her AARP card and her bus pass....hee hee hee!! NANA NOOOOOOOOOO.....!!

Morning Family!

"Metro Talk"....the morning commute has turned into a "Market"....everyone selling anything from candy to jewelry....man taps me and asked if I wanted to buy his bracelet....I ain't even awake yet Dude.....LOL.

Morning Family!

"Metro Talk"……Why when you enter the train or approach a bus stop, ALL eyes are on you, but NO ONE says "Good Morning"? Well I got them....I stepped on the train and said "Morning Dumb Dumbs"....hee hee hee!! A lot of shocked looks and rolling eyes....Was it something I said?...

Morning Family!

"Metro Talk".....You ask me how to get to a destination, I give you the information then you proceed to tell me that it's not the same thing someone else told you!! I ask "Did this other person have a uniform that reads "Metro"?.....NO. Neither do I; good luck with your trip!!

"Metro Talk"…. Okay, at what age do we learn digging in your nose is NASTY? This lady is digging yet drilling her nose like she left her check in that joint....hee hee hee!! Woooooo, yet another Metro story.....

GOOD MORNING FAMILY! :)

"Metro Talk"....this time of year brings alot of tourists to our area, so today a family is riding the train and their daughter is popping, locking and doing some kind of wave with her hands...."So You Think You Can Dance" Sweetie? Not on my feet Punkin, can you move back a little bit? Thank you very much....hee-hee-hee!!!!

"Metro Talk"....what is the deal with folks and these huge backpacks on the subway? Do they realize that every time they turn, they hit or bump someone? Then get an attitude when you bump them back...."Look slim, it's going to be some lunch bags flying up on this train if you bump me again"....hee-hee-hee!!!! Ain't no hiking trails in DC....LMBO!!!

Morning Family! :)

"Metro Talk".....lady with Doctor's lab coat is going from car-to-car on "Green Line" whispering to females while mugging men. She bumps past me twice....I whisper to HER..."U BUMP ME AGAIN AND THERE WILL BE ANOTHER DOCTOR AT THE NEXT STOP FOR YOU".....Good day Dr. Ruth.....hee hee hee!!

Morning Family! :)

"Metro Talk" (Weekend edition)....sitting at Southern Avenue when a dude sits between this lady and myself....I am reading with my head down and I feel this slight vibration of the bench and the lady and I both look up at the same time, then this odor surfaces....Dude passed gas and trying to play it off....LOL. The lady and I look at each other and I SMH....never a dull moment Family....!!

"Metro Talk"....was on the train today and dude next to me was sweating bullets...I guess because it's the middle of summer and he had on a Northface jacket....hee-hee-hee!!! "Man, they calling for t-storms this evening, but you look like you already caught in the rain"....hee-hee-hee!!! Lawd, why do they tempt me so on this darn Metro....!!!

Morning Family! :)

"Metro Talk".....I guess the "Kiss and Ride" at Metro stations is not what it seems.....this dude drops his lady off at Suitland Station, he leans in for a kiss and she smushes his face so hard that his head hits the window......hee hee hee!! That could not have been me because we would have been two face-smushing folks at Suitland Subway Station.....Happy Friday Family!!

"Metro Talk".....must be "Back that Thang Up" Thursday!! Lady squeezing in seat on bus squishing me against window, so I start pushing back!! She looks at me and I say "Excuse me, but this ain't a Luke video, don't keep backing ALL that up on me"....hee hee hee!! She replies "I was just trying to sit down!" GOOD DAY MISS, I SAID "GOOD DAY!"

Morning Family!

"Metro Talk".....I was going to chill today, BUT.....why folks run to seats on the train like we playing musical chairs....LOL. Woman on my heels getting on train so I STOPPED....BOOM, she runs into me. I say, "My bad, did I forget to put my hazards on?....BACK IT UP MISS!!"....Here we go Family....hee hee hee!!

"Metro Talk".....Why do adults carry kid's backpacks? A 300 pound dude carrying a "Sponge Bob" backpack....hee hee hee!! That thing so small looks like a Starburst Candy on his back...!!

Good Morning Family! :)

"Metro Talk"......how are you gonna get on the bus and decide to add money to your SMARTRIP card with a pocket full of change? You got a line of folks behind you and YOU suck your teeth and say "Ya'll gotta chill." Naw Boo, next time you need to take yourself to COINSTAR first .....GOOD DAY MISS, I SAID GOOD DAY....hee hee hee!!

"Metro Talk" WEEKEND EDITION.... Knee-high leather boots, denim shorts and designer jacket...no idea of price! Seeing her trip getting off bus and someone yelling "Should have worn flats"......PRICELESS! HAVE A GOOD WEEKEND FAMILY! :)

"Metro Talk"....lady with all-white ski coat with fur collar snapping at anyone who brushes against her, so I whisper "Cute coat" and she beams "Thank you", so I whisper "How do you keep the collar so clean with a jheri curl?".....hee hee hee!! Look of horror then "crickets".....Good day Miss, I SAID GOOD DAY!!

Morning Family! :)

"Metro Talk".....there should be a mint bowl at the front of bus/train like in restaurants.....person sitting behind me needs an autopsy because something is DEAD in their mouth.....wooooweeeee!! My nostrils are on fire...hee hee hee!! That's the person you don't care if they speak or not, the damage is done breathing.....!!

"Metro Talk"......is it just me or are females wearing the silk caps worn at the hairdresser as accessories now? What the heck? Group of girls get on bus with these caps in various colors that match their outfits.....JANE, GET ME OFF THIS CRAZY THING.....!!

"Metro Talk"......PSA: COVER YOUR MOUTH WHEN YOU YAWN OR SNEEZE!! Dude mouth wide open yawning, so I say "Ewwww, look at that bug" and he nearly chokes trying to close his mouth....hee hee hee!! "Oh, that was some lint, but you might want to cover your mouth for future reference (smirking) and older lady near me winks and smiles.....MY JOB IS DONE HERE!!

Morning Family :)

Words of Encouragement for the Journey

The amazing thing about life is that you choose what you allow into it, what affects you & how you choose to react. HAPPINESS is a choice. Enjoy this day!

Pearls of Wisdom from Genie

I had three interviews today and during one of them, my stomach started growling because I had not eaten breakfast and the interviewer asks "Is that your stomach?"....hee-hee-hee!!! She then says "Boy, you better not pass out in my office" and I replied "If you give me the job, I promise not to come to work hungry".....haaaaaaaaaaaaaaaa!!!! We both shared a good laugh and she said she liked my personality!! LET THE PRAYERS GO UP FAMILY SO THE BLESSINGS CAN COME DOWN :)

Going through this storm is ROUGH and I understand that everything works in God's time, but every now and then I get SCARED and WORRY about where I go from here!!! I beat myself up and worry about whether I am doing enough. Will I land on my feet this time? Thanks for letting me vent Family.....needed to get those thoughts out of my head!!! Like the saying goes "Speak the truth and shame the devil right"?

Have a good night Family :)

God is a GOD OF JUSTICE.....HE has seen every tear you have cried, every hurt and heartbreak, but keep the faith, stand firm on your belief because all that you have gone through has qualified you for DOUBLE. GOD is going to pay you back exceedingly and abundantly beyond your wildest dreams, so don't hold a grudge or dwell in self-pity because of the things you have gone through.....GOD WILL GIVE YOU MORE THAN YOU COULD EVER IMAGINE!! HE IS HANDLING YOUR CASE!! Have a blessed day my Family and know that GOD LOVES YOU AND SO DO I :)

I went to bed worrying about bills, just LIFE SITUATIONS, but today I know that "IT AIN'T OVER UNTIL GOD SAYS IT'S OVER", so I live to fight another day, to move forward with God's grace and mercy and I WILL NOT GIVE UP!!!

Have a blessed and productive day my Family.....LOVE YOU WITH ALL MY HEART :)

Morning Family.....Don't forget those who have helped you get to where you are. Reach back and say "Thank You" because none of us got to where we are by ourselves, so don't make excuses not to see a loved one....have a bigger point of view. Don't be too busy for those God ordained to be in your life. You have something they need....the gift of YOURSELF!! Don't take for granted those God has placed in your life.....let them know how much they mean to you......I SAY TO EACH OF YOU THIS MORNING "THANK YOU"!!! Thank you for loving me, for encouraging me, for uplifting and making me laugh/smile, just for being YOU.

Have a blessed day and know that I love each of you dearly!

Good Morning MY Family,
Make deposits everywhere you go today.....your smile and your kind words can make a difference in someone's day or life!! God places people in our lives for a reason, so use your gifts to make a difference in someone's life today. Let someone know they are appreciated. Take time to tell others what they mean to you. Get your mind off what you don't have and use what you do and God will improve your life for the better!!

LOVE IS NOT LOVE UNTIL YOU GIVE IT AWAY, so today I am telling each and every one of you that I LOVE YOU AND THANK GOD FOR YOUR PRESENCE IN MY LIFE :)

Sometimes God will increase our difficulties to increase our endurance. NO MATTER WHAT WE ARE GOING THROUGH, WE CAN HANDLE IT.....DON'T LET WEARINESS STOP YOU FROM MOVING FORWARD!! Have a blessed day my Family!

FAMILY, YOU ALL know that I am ecstatic right now and I AM SO HUMBLE, GRATEFUL, BLESSED AND HUMBLE AGAIN to ALL of YOU for not only laughing with ME, but LOVING ME, UPLIFTING ME WITH YOUR POSTS and for just being MY FAMILY through this storm....woooooooooooo!!!! Folks have asked me "You shared about being unemployed?" and I replied "Why NOT? This is MY Family, who else would I share MY story with?" :)

ONE THING I KNOW IS "ME" AND I KNOW THAT IF I DON'T "TALK" ABOUT "ME" THEN I AM JUST MAKING NOISE....so many of YOU have told me "THAT THERE IS NO TEST, WITHOUT A TESTIMONY", so here is MY TESTIMONY (fist pumping) I LOVE YOU FAMILY :)

The End….Until Next Time Of Course!

Stay tuned for more

METRO TALK

From the mind of Eugene Hagood!

About the Author

Eugene Hagood is a native Washingtonian through Ft. Washington, MD where he graduated from Oxon Hill High School (Go Clippers…..CLASS OF 1985). He definitely loves music, urban fiction, black romance and mystery novels as well as spending quiet time with friends and family. He currently works in Northern Virginia and attends school at the University of the District of Columbia.

About Kingdom Journey Press

Kingdom Journey Press, Inc. is a full-service publishing company specializing in providing customized services to support our clients from the conception of an idea to getting HIStory to the masses! Since the time of inception and in conjunction with our umbrella organization, Kingdom Journey Enterprises, we have become recognized globally for our ability to establish a unique presence, while building relationships with partners and clients consisting of current and aspiring writers, and ministry, business, and community organizations.

Our services include:

- Manuscript Evaluation
- Coaching for current and aspiring authors
- Editing
- Cover and Print Layout Design
- Print and E-Book Format
- Copyright and Distribution
- Marketing and Sales Support

To contact us and to learn more information about our services, we invite you to visit our website at www.kjpressinc.com.

www.ingramcontent.com/pod-product-compliance
Lightning Source LLC
LaVergne TN
LVHW011211080426
835508LV00007B/727
* 9 7 8 0 9 8 2 7 0 0 1 6 7 *